The Survival of
Muir Woods

by Katherine Talmadge Sallé

Table of Contents

Introduction

Deep forests once covered Earth. Think of how green our planet was! To early humans, the forests seemed endless. They thought the forests would last forever. But they were wrong. Many have disappeared. We used the wood for building supplies and fuel. And we needed the space for cities and farms.

The coast redwood tree was a major member of the ancient North American forest. Today most of those trees are gone. Some have been protected and saved, though. One coast redwood forest that survived is Muir Woods.

The redwood trees in Muir Woods are also some of the oldest living things on earth. Most are between 500 and 800 years old.

An Ancient Forest

Two thousand years ago, redwood forests stretched along the Pacific Coast of North America. Today only about four percent of them remain. These survivors live in a narrow band along the foggy coasts of Oregon and northern California. Part of that forest stands just north of San Francisco. This is Muir Woods.

The **secluded**, or hidden, setting of Muir Woods is a deep **canyon**. In this narrow valley, strong winds cannot **buffet** the redwoods.

Visitors compare Muir Woods to a **cathedral**—a silent, dark church with a very high ceiling. The silence of Muir Woods comes from its green carpet of moss that hushes footsteps. It is dark because the trees grow closely together, shutting out most sunlight. The "high ceiling" comes from the tall redwoods. These are the tallest trees in the world. Most grow to be about 200 to 275 feet (61 to 84 m) tall.

The redwood trees in Muir Woods are ➲ some of the oldest living things on Earth. Most are between 500 and 800 years old.

The Homes of the Coast Miwok

The homes of the Coast Miwok looked somewhat like upside-down ice cream cones. First the Miwok made a tepee-like frame out of fir branches. Then they covered each frame with redwood boards, which they called "kotcha."

The history of this redwood canyon goes back at least 2,000 years. At that time Native Americans called the Coast Miwok lived nearby. The word *Miwok* means "people."

The Miwok came to the redwood canyon on a quest for food. Deep within its walls, they hunted deer and fished for salmon. They also gathered redwood bark and branches to build their homes next to a rocky **cove**.

In 1579 British explorer Sir Francis Drake sailed up the coast. Records suggest that he stopped in the cove to repair his ship. Sketches in the ship's papers show homes like those of the Miwok.

Sir Francis Drake

Two hundred years later, Spanish explorers arrived. The Spanish took over much of the Miwok lands. Then they built their own settlements. In 1838 the Spanish granted land to an American settler, William Richardson. The grant included the redwood canyon.

Until then it had been a place to hunt and fish. However, the nearby town of Yerba Buena was growing. Lumber was needed for buildings and homes. Was the canyon doomed?

CHAPTER 2 Early Challenges

Yerba Buena became San Francisco in 1847. Then gold was discovered nearby in 1848. News spread quickly. By 1849 miners flooded into the region. The population of San Francisco grew from 800 to 25,000 in two years.

All that growth meant more homes. Logging became big business. Lumber ships sailed north for redwood. By 1870 loggers had cut most of the forests near Muir Woods. But the Muir Woods canyon survived. The rocky cove was dangerous for landing ships. Also the steep canyon walls made logging difficult.

The canyon remained as it was. Hikers spread word about its beauty. By the late 1880s, it was popular with horseback riders and campers.

◑ This lumber mill processed the logs that were cut down from the forests near San Francisco.

In 1892 the Bohemian Club, a San Francisco men's club, arrived. Each fall the members went camping. That year they chose to camp in the canyon. They agreed that if they liked it, they would buy it. Then they would build a campsite that would last.

Before the trip they built a huge statue of Buddha in the woods. The night of their campout was cold and damp. They decided not to buy Muir Woods. Instead they bought another redwood grove in a warmer place. Again the woods were left alone.

By 1900 logging tools and methods had advanced. It would now be easier to cut and haul the canyon's trees. People became concerned about the forest. How long would it remain as it was?

The Buddha of Bohemian Grove

The Bohemian Club built their Buddha out of wood and plaster. They left it in place after their camping trip. Gradually the damp fog made it fall apart. By the 1920s, it was gone. Today the **grove** where it once stood is called Bohemian Grove.

⋒ William Kent is the man on the left.

A **conservationist** named William Kent became concerned about the forest. He wanted to preserve, or save, the forest. As a businessman, he wanted to make money. He thought he might profit by bringing tourists in. But the land cost $45,000. His wife said that was too much. He agreed. But then he visited the forest again. "The beauty of the place attracted me," he later wrote. His wife remained against it. But this time Kent disagreed. "If we lost all the money we have, and saved those trees, it would be worthwhile," he told her. In 1905 he bought it.

CHAPTER 3 Friends of the Forest

Kent bought the forest just in time. One year later a dreadful earthquake rocked San Francisco. Much of the city burned to the ground. Lumber was badly needed to rebuild. Had the forest still been for sale, it surely would have been chopped down.

But Kent had other plans. A train took tourists up nearby Mt. Tamalpais. Kent made a deal with the owners. They would build track into his canyon to bring tourists in. He would build an inn where they could stay. They would both make money. The owners eagerly agreed.

⋔ The new railway line was called "the crookedest railroad in the world," because of its windy path up the mountain and down into Kent's canyon.

Then Kent faced a new challenge. The San Francisco earthquake and fires had frightened the public. They demanded a new, larger supply of water. A water company responded with a plan. They would dam Redwood Creek for a **reservoir**. Such a move would drown the forest.

Kent searched for ways to save it. Then he learned that Congress had passed a new law in 1906, the Antiquities Act. With it the president could save lands "of historic or scientific interest." President Roosevelt turned out to be just the friend the redwoods needed.

Theodore Roosevelt, Friend of the American Wilderness

Theodore Roosevelt became president in 1901. While in office he set aside 148 million acres of forest reserves. He also created 5 national parks and set aside 50 wildlife preserves. Under the Antiquities Act of 1906, he created 18 national monuments. One of the first was Kent's redwood canyon.

On January 9, 1908, Roosevelt declared the redwood canyon a National Monument. That protected it. No one could cut it, flood it, or buy it. It belonged to all American citizens.

Roosevelt wanted to name the forest Kent's Woods. But Kent had a better idea. He chose the name Muir Woods, to honor America's greatest conservationist.

⋂ John Muir at Muir Woods

John Muir loved nature. He once walked a thousand miles, just to be outdoors. As a young man, he had a bad accident and almost went blind. That's when he made himself a promise. If he regained his sight, he would spend his life enjoying the sights of nature. His eyesight returned. So he sailed to San Francisco. At the dock, he asked a man for directions. "Where do you want to go?" the man asked.

"Any place that is wild," Muir said.

Muir found his wild places. He especially loved the Sierra Mountains and redwood forests. He fought hard to save the trees and the land. He also wrote books to persuade others to join the fight. Then, in 1892, he helped form the Sierra Club. He was its first president.

Kent's idea was perfect. And John Muir was delighted. He wrote this letter to Kent.

February 6, 1908

Dear Mr. Kent:

Seeing my name in the tender and deed of the Tamalpais Sequoias was a surprise of the pleasantest kind. This is the best tree-lover's monument that could possibly be found in all the forests of the world. You have done me great honor and I am proud of it.

Saving these woods from the axe and saw, from money-changer and water changers, and giving them to our country and world is in many ways the most notable service to God and man I've heard of since my forest wanders began. . . .

Ever yours,

John Muir

4  Modern History

William Kent was elected to Congress in 1910. In 1916 he introduced a bill that formed the National Park Service. Its two **missions** were to **conserve** wild lands and insure the public's enjoyment of them.

At first enjoyment tended to hamper conservation. There were few rules. People **trampled** the moss and ferns. They dug up wildflowers. They even burned campfires. Muir Woods was a mess.

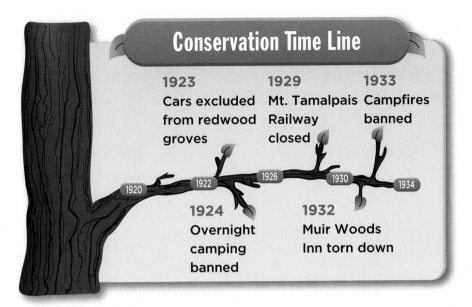

Conservation Time Line

1923
Cars excluded from redwood groves

1929
Mt. Tamalpais Railway closed

1933
Campfires banned

1924
Overnight camping banned

1932
Muir Woods Inn torn down

1920 1922 1926 1930 1934

⌒ In the 1920s and 1930s, steps were taken to reduce the damage to Muir Woods.

New rules helped Muir Woods. But the crowds increased. Until 1937 ferries brought most tourists from San Francisco. Then a new bridge opened. The Golden Gate increased the flow of cars.

In 1942 Muir Woods got a new ranger, Lawson Brainerd. When he arrived, 14 footbridges crossed Redwood Creek. He reduced them to 4. He also removed the picnic tables. Then he fenced the trails.

Brainerd's efforts worked. Muir Woods slowly changed. It was becoming a safe place for ancient trees.

☾ Lawson Brainerd fenced the trails to prevent people from walking on the moss and ferns.

In 1945 World War II ended. In May many world leaders came to San Francisco. Their mission was to form the United Nations. President Franklin D. Roosevelt was to lead the event. Sadly he died in April. The world leaders signed the United Nations charter. Then they came to Muir Woods. In a redwood grove, they held a ceremony. Here are the words on a plaque they installed.

Here in this grove of enduring redwoods, preserved for **posterity**, members of the United Nations Conference on International Organization met on May 19, 1945, to honor the memory of Franklin Delano Roosevelt, thirty-first president of the United States, chief architect of the United Nations and apostle of peace for all mankind.

There are other plaques in Muir Woods. William Kent had a favorite tree. He didn't choose a redwood, though. He chose a stately Douglas fir. Kent died in 1928, but his tree lives on. The William Kent Tree is now almost 400 years old. And in 1976, one tree became the Bicentennial Tree. To honor our nation's two hundredth birthday, the park rangers chose a tree that was also 200.

Conclusion

By 1900 many redwood forests were gone. Some trees were cut for valuable lumber. Others were cleared for new towns and farms. But Muir Woods survived. Early on, its remote location saved it from lumber crews. Later on, important friends stepped in to help.

Muir Woods is beautiful today. However, it is still a "recovering forest." The goal of the National Park Service is to put it back to its original state.

Muir Woods is once again becoming the **habitat** of woodland creatures. The brown bears and grizzlies are gone, but the bobcats, deer, and fox have returned. So have the salmon and trout. And each summer legions of ladybugs migrate to Muir Woods and form huge clusters, in the same spots year after year.

Muir Woods is open every day, from early morning until sunset. Visit and look up as high as you can. You will never be able to see all the way to the tops of those ancient redwood trees. But the trees are survivors. They will remain.

↑ Owls have returned to Muir Woods.

Glossary

buffet *(BUF-it)* to beat or thrust about, as by the force of strong winds *(page 4)*

canyon *(CAN-yun)* a long, narrow valley between high cliffs, often with a stream flowing through it *(page 4)*

cathedral *(kuh-THEE-druhl)* a large and important church *(page 4)*

conserve *(con-SERV)* to save and protect natural resources such as water, land, and trees from harm or waste *(page 16)*

conservationist *(con-ser-VAY-shun-ist)* a person who works to conserve natural resources *(page 11)*

cove *(KOHV)* a small sheltered bay or inlet *(page 6)*

grove *(GROHV)* a group of trees standing together *(page 10)*

habitat *(HAB-i-tat)* the region where a plant or animal naturally grows or lives *(page 21)*

mission *(MISH-uhn)* a job or commitment *(page 16)*

posterity *(po-STAYR-i-tee)* future generations *(page 18)*

reservoir *(REZ-ur-vwar)* a natural or artificial lake in which water is stored and reserved for use *(page 13)*

secluded *(suh-KLOOD-ed)* shut off or kept apart from others; hidden or isolated *(page 4)*

trample *(TRAM-puhl)* to crush or destroy by the feet of people or animals *(page 16)*

Index

Comprehension Check

Summarize

Outline each section of *The Survival of Muir Woods*. List each chapter and write its main idea. Then list two or three key ideas from each chapter. Include examples that illustrate each one. Compare and contrast Muir Woods to other forests.

Think and Compare

1. Look at page 4. The author suggests similarities and differences between a cathedral and Muir Woods. Tell how they are alike and different. *(Compare and Contrast)*

2. Think of a natural place—such as a field, a park, or a forest—that you enjoy. What might you do to protect it and keep it clean and healthy? *(Apply)*

3. A few people did special things to save Muir Woods. Which "friend of the forest" do you think gave the greatest amount of help? Explain your point of view. *(Evaluate)*